The Scars on my heart and brain

Nicolas Amaro

BookLeaf Publishing

Presentation by *BookLeaf Publishing*

Web: www.bookleafpub.com

E-mail: info@bookleafpub.com

ISBN : 9789357699181

First edition 2022

DEDICATION

To Mom, Rory, Conner, Brenda, and Sunnie.
You've been a special part of my life without you I don't know where I'd be.
I love you all.

ACKNOWLEDGEMENT

I'd like to acknowledge those who have been in my life whether it was good or bad it made an impact on me and who I am now.

PREFACE

I am writing this to gain some better understanding of myself. I was diagnosed with autism as an adult and later depression and anxiety disorder to top off with Insomnia. I have had Time to write a lot of what's on my mind and how I release my emotions.

Soul song

Should I live knowing that things might not be fulfilled? Why do I persist to find the things that only break my heart? My broken spirit cries out for what I cannot obtain. To be held and know what real love could be. My heart longs to hold you. A ripple within a tidal wave cannot be felt. I try to smile while I sing my soul song to my inspiration.

Without my inspiration I may as well lay in bed without any will to leave. The loneliness is crippling. The same dream plays in my mind. Another day goes by where the world goes on without me. I want to find a way to carry on. So at the dock I sit and sing my soul song.

Lost in thought

I see you across the room
Or eyes lock on each other
Flashes of love hit like a sonic boom
No need to duck and cover
Rational thought is out the door
I have to talk to you
Like nothing I've felt before
And I have to see if it's true
Can you fall in love at first sight?
Or is it a myth?
If it takes all night
I wish for a kiss you'll have with this wordsmith
Dreaming of what could be
An entire what if scenario plays in my head
If you could only see
A moment in time but I'm frozen instead
And now you're smiling at me
As I see you walk away
But before you leave
I have to run to you and say
What's your name?
What's your sign?
Would you feel the same?
Would you be mine?

Kryptonite

The words you speak are heartfelt
From your lips to my ears my heart melts
To know you personally a thought comes to
mind
Your voice and beauty I've never seen before
I close my eyes and see only your face
I'd wish to see it forever and that's no mistake
The thought of you and my heart skips a beat
To hold you in my arms in the summer heat
I want explain to you but I'm unable to speak
Getting close to you gets my knees weak
Longing to touch and kiss you in the moonlight
I'm not sure if it's fear or maybe my kryptonite

Weak

You've brought out something in me
I can't really explain it
I get so weak in the knee
But I won't try to sit
Because I will walk 1000 miles to you
I've lost all control
If you're near I know what to do
I can feel it in my soul
My heart beats triple time
Whenever you are close
Hell even if you're on my mind
Stay with me you won't impose
I'll swallow my pride
To tell you how I feel
I want you by my side
Even while our hearts heal
You're always on my brain
You knock me of my feet
I'll never be the same
I can't explain why your love makes me weak

Unloved

All I do is hide
The anger I feel inside
The hurt and the pain
For a while I haven't been the same
Hearts been broke
There's no hope
Mending slowly in solitude
Not too forgiving and twice as rude
Hiding deep inside
Feels for one I haven't seen in a long time
Is she still out there?
Would she even care?
That I've been broken
And become soft spoken
Insomnia and anxiety fill my mind
Looking for something I can never find
I'll never feel like I'm good enough
Love is always tough
No matter how hard I try
I'm alone and I know why
Maybe one day I won't be
Until that happens we'll see

Expendable

What is even the point?
when all you do is disappoint
I've felt alone too long
and maybe its just time to be gone
maybe I'm blinded by anger
but you've become a stranger
I cancel plans to put you first
But you bail on me and make it worse
you have me upset but don't know why
because you'll hang with your friends and lie
and I just don't care anymore
cause you'll lie like before
do I deserve this?
is karmic retribution taking what was bliss?
it might be that but why even bother?
in this relationship I'm just fodder
shattered my heart and lost my soul
now I'll walk away with this gaping hole
fill it with anger to get through the day
because it's pointless to ask you to stay
no point in finding another
it'll be awhile before I find another lover

Don’t let the sun go down on me

Too late I can't help but fall
Taking a chance, risking it all
Can't let the sun go down on me
Let it shine on us and what we can be
I can't help how I feel
Let the cuts on my heart finally heal
We can live oh so free
Just don't let the sun go down on me
It's hard to find the words to say
That I can't be without you another day
Your smile is so bright
And every kiss feels just right
Stay in my arms
Because I will never mean you harm
Without you I don't know where I can be
Losing you is like the sun going down on me

In The Dark

I was in the dark
But you lit up my heart
I know it's hard to show
But I just want you to know
I keep quiet because I'm scared
Afraid of a life without you there
My heart still beats for you
Even though we've split in two
When my fear became reality
Life just became harder for me
The light is flickering to stay on
And I don't like what I've become
Alone, cold, and distant
The darkness takes over unassisted
Lost in my mind
Looking for love I will never really find
Fight the emptiness creeping out
Battling the never ending self doubt
I will find my happiness in due time
Holding on for real love to be mine

In my head

I spent these last few months feeling worthless
Working more and social less
Never pertaining to being useful
So I am used to being told that I'm a fool
So I started to think that I would better off dead
With my finger on the trigger and all I can say is
go
ahead
No flash of light no voice of god telling me to
stop
Just the look on my loved ones faces if they
knew
that I had been shot
Tears run down my cheeks and the moment
comes to pass
I've ruined myself because I can't run from my
past
I push everyone away because I don't like what I
have to say
Trying to make myself tough because I never
feel
like I'm good enough
But you tell me I am and what it's worth to be
alive
Overcoming this depression has been but I will
try

I know that I may have strained the relationship
But I hope that in time I can mend it
Believe in me like I believe in love
And it won't be perfect nor the way it was.

The one

What was on my mind in that last rhyme
I had been holding in for a long time
The woman I spoke of then
I haven't seen again
She made this man smile when all was lost
We took care of each other no matter the cost
No matter what problem we faced
We handled it together post haste
When she left everything hurt so bad
And all the time I was feeling so mad
The pain in my heart hasn't stopped
So I'll try to ignore it without a second thought
Our time together was the best of my life
Even though now I only feel strife
I say these things as a cautionary tale
If you let go of love it is bound to fail
Will I be fine again? Only time will tell
Swearing off love isn't going so well
The emptiness is a gaping hole
And I long to regain control
I let the sun go down on me
I look in the mirror and don't know who I see
Like the story of Job
I've almost lost all hope
Whenever I hear the words patience and time
I think back to her and my earlier rhyme

Here with me

I didn't think you cared
With the moments that we shared
And I don't want to lose a thing
With all the joy you bring
And it might be hard to see
But you'll forever be in my memory
Missing each other everyday
And somehow we find a way
It's hard to breathe
Until I know you're here with me
I now know deep down
You feel what I've been feeling all around
This new found feeling can't subside
And I don't want it to hide
We can both run free
As long as you're here with me
I didn't know you cared back
But it's enough about that
I see what's under the tough exterior
I see a heart that's beyond superior
One the hasn't loved in a while
Be the one to bring in romantic styles
Everything you want and need
As long as you're here with me

The only one

There's something I want you to know
8
There are things I need to say before I go
because
I'm haunted by the past
So listen closely cause it'll be fast
I'm in love with you, cutting to the chase
After a long time I'm telling you face to face
Cause you showed kindness more than anyone
I couldn't live up to that, look what I've become
I've made mistakes my entire life
Being with you always felt so right
I've held onto these feelings for many years
It wasn't fair to keep inside due to fear
When I dream it's about life with you
Now I have the chance to make them come true
I know this wasn't written in your plans
Just lead the way and I'll take your hands
There's nowhere I'd rather be
Only if you decide to take a chance on me
Couldn't hide you from the truth
About how much I cared since our you
Give it a chance to start a new
Because I only wanna be with you

Love is a crime

Love should be a crime
I see it happen all the time
All of my heart and my mind
For someone like you that's hard to find
You wanted it to end tonight
And it didn't feel right
It took so much to force the words out
But your heart wanted to shout
The tears coming from your eyes
While your words came as a surprise
Holding you I will forever miss
The feel of your lips whenever we kiss
Happiness has paid its fine
Love should be a crime
What I've felt for you
Had been around longer than you knew
How you felt could never be confirmed
So my feelings were on the back burner
Now I'm sitting here sad and blue
Because I can't picture life without you
Trips anywhere feel pointless
I'd rather have you in my arms to confess
The pain inside is hard to define
Love should be a crime

Will you be there?

If everything fell apart in my world
And there is trouble
Will you stay my girl?
Or will you leave the bubble?
I need to know
With all my heart and soul
Will you still care?
Are you gonna be there?
Don't say love should be a crime
When this is a love of a lifetime
I'll meet you anywhere
But I need to know are you gonna be there?
Help me see the light
When being with you feels right
Will you be mine?
Because we've got love on our side
If times get hard will you be there to hold?
Or will you leave me out in the cold?
Will you be in my world?
Because you're the only girl
The choice will be yours
The answer will have me shaking to my core
When I need someone beside me
Only you can see
We'll only be fair..
But my question is are you gonna be there?

The loneliness

Now I am walking alone
It feels the darkness taking control
I see loneliness again
My old friend where do I begin
Take a wild guess
I somehow managed to make a mess
A great love has been lost
By my own hand, the worst cost
I don't think I can ever be alright
As I go through another lonely night
Wishing I was dead inside
So I won't have to keep drying my eyes
But truth be told you brought this light
You've made this lonely heart burn bright
I won't sit here and reminisce
About what it is about you that I miss
It's hard to accept the fact
That there is no way back
You've helped me become the man I am now
And at the moment the silence won't show me how
How do I go on when the best part of me is gone?
What do I do now that life has played like a sad song?

Nothing makes sense
I guess I'll give in to the loneliness

Young love

Try to make love last
Forgetting about the past
The innocence you had felt
Enough to make their heart melt
And you can't turn back
Falling in love might give myself a heart attack
Looking at our photographs
I remember when our young hearts would beat fast
On the road of life
Stop to look around and don't think twice
Can't go back to how it used to be
If you were friends now it's for fate to see
Your young hearts can take the trials
Loving you in all romantic stylez
True love can trump all
If you're ready to take that fall
Something like that takes work
But it pays off proving your worth
Together we can live
With all I have to give
And I can't bear the reason why
If young love dies
I won't let us drift apart
Giving to all to Young hearts

My Paper Heart

Holding on to old love isn't good for me
It eats at me without making a sound
Drowning in the middle of the Sea
Hopelessness weighing me down
Swimming in the tears left behind by you
Washing away any part of me you held dear
You don't know what I'm going through
Despite what others might hear
I desperately hold on to you
Memories play in my head like a video
Hurt makes my paper heart rip apart
Your voice plays in stereo
And the ocean of despair isn't too far
I tried to say goodbye and couldn't find the words
If there was something else I could've said
But alas I didn't have the courage
And now the scenario plays in my head
The only love I ever wanted
The only one I need
And now I am haunted
And my paper heart will bleed

Mr. Hyde

The days pass by
And I wonder where I went wrong
I can't make things right
And I listen to sad songs
When you think you have it all
But reality sinks in
And everything is going to fall
You will never win
Crying isn't the only way
And now you're alone
And the drugs comes through the fray
So you're nowhere near your phone
The monster caused so many problems
And slowly takes control
And now you're hurting them
And losing your soul
When you're mind escapes the despair
And no one is around
Now life doesn't seem fair
And you've hit the ground
No words can describe the pain
And I chosen to isolate
I wish that it would rain
Cause I can't escape fate

My love song

Home is wherever I'm with you
Before love there were things I never knew
And the song plays in my heart
And I'm better once it starts
When I'm alone without you
I forget about what to do
I find it hard to see
The feeling of joy that you bring me
You captivate me entirely
So I can become the man I'm meant to be
It doesn't matter what anyone will say or do
I will always love you
In moments where things don't seem wrong
I look to you and hear my love song
When you look in my eyes
You see passed the drugs and the lies
It's comforting to feel whole again
I just want to hold you now and then
Slow down the the clock
Just love you whole time stops
Together while the days are long
Baby you are my love song

Life Lesson

I regret every mistake I ever made
But things will never be the same
I hoped that things would be different
But all the green lights went red
And it seems life has cut the brakes
I know I'm not going to be safe
I might be losing my sanity
Or maybe losing my humanity
While I'm bracing for impact
I see the things leading to the fact
I've held on to all the heartbreak
My soul has layered it like cake
It's got me feeling undeserving
I've let the darkness continue covering
As I'm crashing I feel enveloped by the light
I'm at peace and everything feels alright
And a voice tells me I have to go
Things aren't finished for you don't you know?
The pain inside has to dissipate
It's almost consumed you whole it would be too late
Forgive yourself for the hurt you caused
And live the life you almost tossed
Work your way back
Now brace for impact
Waking up in a bed my body intact

Looking up not feeling the same
I cry to ease my pain
Lesson here is love and life find a way
Never give up if you think it's over, stay

Outrunning the Past

I spent these last few months feeling worthless
Working more and social less
Never pertaining to being useful
So I am used to being told that I'm a fool
So I started to think that I would better off dead
With my finger on the trigger and all I can say is
go
ahead
No flash of light no voice of god telling me to
stop
Just the look on my loved ones faces if they
knew
that I had been shot
Tears run down my cheeks and the moment
comes to pass
I've ruined myself because I can't run from my
past
I push everyone away because I don't like what I
have to say
Trying to make myself tough because I never
feel
like I'm good enough
But you tell me I am and what it's worth to be
alive
Overcoming this depression has been but I will
try

I know that I may have strained the relationship
But I hope that in time I can mend it
Believe in me like I believe in love
And it won't be perfect nor the way it was.

www.ingramcontent.com/pod-product-compliance
Lightning Source LLC
Chambersburg PA
CBHW051753130826
49812CB00033B/1124
* 9 7 8 9 3 5 7 6 9 9 1 8 1 *